ROY PASCAL AND GEORG LUKÁCS

TOWARDS A RE-EVALUATION OF THE HISTORY OF MARXIST LITERARY CRITICISM IN BRITAIN?

Helmut Peitsch

THE 2017 BITHELL MEMORIAL LECTURE

Institute of Modern Languages Research
School of Advanced Study, University of London

2018

Published by the

INSTITUTE OF MODERN LANGUAGES RESEARCH

School of Advanced Study, University of London
Senate House, Malet Street, London WC1E 7HU

https://modernlanguages.sas.ac.uk

Cover images:
Georg Lukács, 1952 (Bundesarchiv, Bild 183–15304–0097_CC-BY-SA)
Roy Pascal (from a personal collection)

First published 2018

ISBN 978 0 85457 267 0
ISSN 0144-9850

INTRODUCTION

We are delighted to welcome Professor Helmut Peitsch to the Institute of Modern Languages Research – and to present the 2017 Bithell Memorial Lecture. Not only is he one of the most distinguished Germanists today, Helmut Peitsch also has a long-standing connection with the Institute. He is one of our Corresponding Members and a few years ago, gave a fascinating talk here on the London branch of the German PEN-Zentrum, which, founded in 1933 by Jewish émigrés from the Hitler regime, continued to exist until 2002. He has lived and worked both in Britain and in Germany – and this double allegiance to German and British academia has contributed to a broader approach to the discipline, an ability to see and combine different perspectives, and a refusal to think in terms of separate – or even hierarchical – understandings of 'Inlands- and Auslandsgermanistik'.

In introducing Professor Peitsch to you, I should just like to highlight a few of the landmarks, achievements and publications that define his career. He began his professional life at the German department of the Freie Unversität Berlin, where he had also been a student. It was here that his interest in – and acute awareness of – the interplay between politics and literature was fostered, an interest and indeed an *approach* that has characterized his entire body of research. He took up lectureships in Leeds and Swansea, then professorial posts at New York University and at Cardiff, and since 2001, has been Professor of Modern German Literature (now emeritus) at the University of Potsdam.

Professor Peitsch's main publications – and I shall have to be very selective here – fall into two distinct areas of research. The first of these is the exploration of the works, thought and influence of the eighteenth-century philosopher, travel writer and 'Weltbürger' Georg Forster. Volumes on Forster's Humanist thinking and his ideas of revolutionary democracy, on his critical reception, and – very recently (2017) on Forster's writings on Germany's 'participation' in Europe's expansion into the non-European world testify to Helmut Peitsch's in-depth engagement with this thinker.

The second of his main areas of research is post-Second World War German literature, the writing of the 'Nachkriegsjahre' in East and West Germany. Two publications stand out here: *Vom Faschismus zum Kalten Krieg. Auch eine deutsche Literaturgeschichte. Literaturverhältnisse, Genres, Themen* (1996), and *Nachkriegsliteratur 1945–1989* (2009). Both volumes question narratives of a 'tradition of German literature', and in particular the idea of a 'Nationalliteratur'. They remind readers of the conditions of canon formation – and of texts that have not made it into that canon. In outlining the history of the origins and transformations of the *two* German literatures that developed after – and in opposition to – fascism, Professor Peitsch pays particular attention to the political and material circumstances and constraints under which these literatures were shaped and operated. A third book also belongs to this field of enquiry: entitled *No Politics?* (please note the question mark!), it is *Die Geschichte des deutschen PEN-Zentrums in London 1933–2002* (2006). Here literature is again analysed in its interrelationship with politics, institutional systems and market forces.

Helmut Peitsch is senior advisor to the Zentrum für Jüdische Studien in Berlin, and his work has contributed to German-Jewish literary history in a major way. He is currently working – among other things – on a history of the descriptions of Auschwitz in travel writing. The word 'retirement' doesn't seem to have much meaning for him.

The 2017 Bithell Memorial Lecture is entitled 'Roy Pascal and Georg Lukács: Towards a Re-evaluation of the History of Marxist Literary Criticism in Britain?'. I am very grateful to Professor Peitsch for suggesting this topic, as it is one that is close to the heart of Germanists in this country. Many of us have been brought up on Roy Pascal's 1956 book on the German novel; some of us knew him personally, were taught by him, or worked with him, and he gave the Bithell Memorial Lecture in 1977. Pascal was influential in our field – not only because of his position (he was Professor of German at Birmingham for some thirty years) – but because of his approach to literature and his personality. For him, literature was firmly related not only to the historical context in which it originated, but also to its philosophical underpinning and to its moral aspirations and implications.

It is easy to see the line connecting Lukács via Roy Pascal to Helmut Peitsch: a tradition of combining a political with an aesthetic interest when looking at literature – a tradition of critical and dialectical reading, questioning any narratives that promise too smooth and 'natural' a grand arch, a tradition of precise analysis and of great personal commitment and integrity.

Dr Godela Weiss-Sussex
London, October 2017

ROY PASCAL AND GEORG LUKÁCS: TOWARDS A RE-EVALUATION OF THE HISTORY OF MARXIST LITERARY CRITICISM IN BRITAIN?

At the 150th anniversary conference of Germanists in Frankfurt in 1996, Eda Sagarra, Professor of Germanic Studies at Trinity College Dublin, referred to Roy Pascal as 'one of the most influential British Germanists in general': 'His work [...] is still effective as always. His books on autobiography and narrative forms [...] are pioneering works'.[1] However, this evaluation was only printed as a footnote in the proceedings of the conference at which Eda Sagarra presented her paper entitled 'Die britische Germanistik 1896 bis 1946'.[2] The footnote suggests an explanation for a statement in the main text: 'He remained [...] until the 1960s a bit of an outsider, influential for the time being only on the youth', asserting that he was a 'member of the British Communist Party until 1956'.[3] Five years before Eda Sagarra's comment, Rodney Livingstone, writing about 'The Contribution of German-speaking Jewish Refugees to German Studies in Britain', referred to Pascal as part of 'a small, but articulate "Left wing" in German Studies, ably represented by Roy Pascal, who wrote a book critical of Nazism as early as 1934'.[4] Illustrating one of the lasting contributions of German-speaking Jewish immigrants to German Studies in Britain, namely '[t]he introduction of interdisciplinary or comparative studies', Livingstone referred to one of Pascal's pupils, Siegbert Salomon Prawer and his *Karl Marx and World Literature*, and returning to Pascal stated: 'The concern with German thought was of course not the monopoly of the immigrants. We may point to Pascal's work in this area which goes back to the 1930s.' These differing assessments of Pascal's work as a Germanist hint at the problems of positioning Marxist literary criticism within German Studies in Britain: was Roy Pascal a left-winger in, or an outsider to academic German Studies? Did he carry out pioneering research from 1934 or only after 1960? Neither evaluation uses the term 'Marxist' to characterize Pascal's literary criticism from the 1930s to the 1950s. Pascal's

1 Eda Sagarra, 'Die britische Germanistik 1896 bis 1946', in *Zur Geschichte und Problematik der Nationalphilologien in Europa. 150 Jahre Erste Germanistenversammlung in Frankfurt am Main (1846–1996)*, ed. by Frank Fürbeth et al. (Tübingen: Niemeyer, 1999), pp. 683–96 (p. 691). All translations of German quotations into English are my own.

2 Sagarra, 'Die britische Germanistik 1896 bis 1946', p. 691.

3 Sagarra, 'Die britische Germanistik 1896 bis 1946', p. 691.

4 Rodney Livingstone, 'The Contribution of German-speaking Jewish Refugees to German Studies in Britain', in *Second Chance: Two Centuries of German-speaking Jews in the United Kingdom*, ed. by Werner Mosse (Tübingen: Mohr, 1991), pp. 137–51 (p. 144).

biographers have so far been silent as to his relations with the work of the most prominent international representative of Marxist literary criticism of the period, Georg Lukács, overlooking that Pascal wrote the 'Foreword' to Lukács's *Studies in European Realism* which appeared in 1950. But they were not the only ones to contribute to this kind of silence. By bringing in British Marxists who were not Germanists, I would like to expand the field of enquiry to enable a re-evaluation of Marxist literary criticism in Britain. The critic Walter Allen, in his 1950 article in *New Statesman and Nation*, reviewed Lukács's *Studies in European Realism* as 'recently done into what is often English' [*sic*] though 'written in a tradition quite different from, indeed alien to, any that the great majority of English critics inhabit'.[5]

In 1962, for the first time, a collection of essays by Georg Lukács appeared in the Federal Republic of Germany. Published in Luchterhand's 'Sociological Texts' series and entitled *Writings on the Sociology of Literature*, it was edited by the sociologist Peter Christian Ludz. Reviewing this collection in the Hamburg weekly *Die Zeit*, Peter Demetz, the Yale Germanist and Comparatist from Prague, reminded his West German readers: 'In England, a collection of Lukács's most important articles has been available for some time which open up a first view of his world, edited by Professor Roy Pascal; after some delay, the Federal Republic is finally catching up on this Anglosaxon lead.'[6]

Forty years later, however, when in 2002, Eric Hobsbawm remembered the 'Interesting Times' of the mid-twentieth century – in the German translation 'Gefährliche Zeiten', i.e. 'dangerous times' – he reflected on what 'helped to anglicize my way of thinking': 'What Perry Anderson has called "western Marxism", the Marxism of Lukács, the Frankfurt School and Korsch, never crossed the Channel until the 1960s.'[7] Although Hobsbawm remembered 'the superb Germanist' Roy Pascal in the chapter on Cambridge as 'one of the rare communist dons',[8] he did not mention that in 1950, the same year that Pascal had written the foreword to Georg Lukács's *Studies in European Realism*, Hobsbawm himself had provided the introduction to Jozsef Révai's *Lukács & Socialist Realism. A Hungarian Literary Controversy*.[9]

In the same year, 1962, that Peter Demetz reminded West German readers

5   Walter Allen, 'A Review of Lukács's *Studies in European Realism*' (*New Statesman and Nation*, 40, 22 July 1950, 100–01 (p. 100).

6   Peter Demetz, 'Eine Gestalt zwischen den Drahtverhauen. Georg Lukács, bald verschrien, bald zum Schutzheiligen erhoben', *Die Zeit*, 6 April 1962.

7   Eric Hobsbawm, *Interesting Times. A Twentieth-Century Life* (London: Abacus, 2002 [1st edn.]), p. 97.

8   Hobsbawm, *Interesting Times*, p. 112.

9   Compare however the opening paper of the *1985 Delhi Seminar* on Lukács: 'I remember that in the first week of January 1950 I bought the book *Studies in European Realism* translated

of the 1950 publication of *Studies in European Realism*, Raymond Williams reminded readers of *The Listener* that '[*The Historical Novel*] is the second book by Georg Lukács [...] to appear in English. A translation of *Studies in European Realism* appeared in 1950.'[10] Williams did not name Roy Pascal. But Williams's 'Notes on Marxism in Britain since 1945' which came out in 1977, the same year that Pascal was to deliver his Bithell Memorial Lecture, suggest an explanation: Williams places 'a decisive insertion [...] of Marxism into a range of strictly academic work' 'in the academic expansion of the sixties and early seventies'.[11] Prior to this, 'until 1960 and beyond [Marxism] was very generally regarded as un-English, irrelevant and irremediably out-of-date',[12] '[u]ntil 1956 [...] there was a simple general equation between Marxism and the ideological position of the Communist Party'.[13] On an autobiographical note Williams stresses the kind of import of Marxist cultural theory which followed from this situation: 'received Marxist [cultural] theory (which I began by accepting)' 'came through not only as Engels and Plekhanov, [...] but as Zhdanov'.[14]

'Pascal introduced the British readers to the reading of Lukács' – the Cardiff historian Kevin Morgan states in his contribution to a recent volume on the relations of the Socialist Unity Party of Germany (SED) to Communist Parties of Western and Southern Europe;[15] Morgan's title alludes to Pascal's very first publication in German, *Deutschland – Weg und Irrweg*.[16] This German version of Pascal's *The Growth of Modern Germany*[17] was the very

---

by Edith Bone with a foreword by Roy Pascal, and I still have it. That was the first book by Lukács which people here saw. And it is noteworthy that when this book was published for the first time in London, it was not by Lawrence and Wishart but by some unknown Hillway Publishing Company, London. It is possible that Lawrence and Wishart did not publish the book because of the ongoing controversy.' (Namwar Singh, 'Lukács and Hindi Literary Criticism', in *Contributions on Lukács. Papers of the 1985 Delhi Seminar*, ed. by Margit Köves and Shaswati Mazumdar (New Delhi: Department of Slavonic and Finno-Ugrian Studies and Hungarian Information and Cultural Centre, 1989), vol. 2, pp. 1–16.

10   Raymond Williams, 'From Scott to Tolstoy', *The Listener*, 67, 1962, 436–37 (p. 436).

11   Raymond Williams, 'Notes on Marxism in Britain since 1945', *New Left Review*, 100, November 1976/January 1977, 81–94 (p. 84).

12   Williams, 'Notes on Marxism', p. 81.

13   Williams, 'Notes on Marxism', p. 82.

14   Williams, 'Notes on Marxism', p. 88.

15   Kevin Morgan, 'Ein besonderer Weg oder ein Irrweg? Britische Kommunisten und die KPD/SED als stalinistisches Beispiel', in *Bruderparteien jenseits des Eisernen Vorhangs: die Beziehungen der SED zu den kommunistischen Parteien West- und Südeuropas (1968–1989)*, ed. by Arnd Bauerkämper and Francesco di Palma (Berlin: Links, 2011), pp. 103–22 (p. 113).

16   Roy Pascal, *Deutschland – Weg und Irrweg* (Berlin: Volk und Welt, 1947).

17   Roy Pascal, *The Growth of Modern Germany* (London: Cobbett Press, 1946).

first translation from the English language to be published by Volk und Welt, the East German publisher specializing in foreign literature.[18] Even before the translation appeared, the SED's daily *Neues Deutschland* had published a sharp criticism of a previous review essay on 'English Books on Germany'; the economist Jürgen Kuczynski who had returned to Berlin from exile in Britain as one of the first German communists was outraged 'that the unique, new, progressive book on German history which appeared in England, that by Roy Pascal, has not been mentioned at all'.[19] A year after Pascal's book on Germany had come out in German, it appeared together with Jürgen Kuczynski's *Monopolists and Junkers*[20] on a list of twenty-two books which the Military Government had banned from distribution in bookshops in Lower Saxony,[21] though not in other parts of the British Zone of Occupation. Pascal and Kuczynski were the only authors banned who were not professional politicians – such as Lenin, Molotov, Ulbricht and Grotewohl.[22]

The banning of the British author's book in (a part of) British-occupied Germany raises the question of the exclusion of Marxism from British post-war culture for which Eric Hobsbawm referred to Perry Anderson. Raymond Williams insisted in his 'Notes' that after 1960 British Cultural Studies did not emerge 'as a critique within a theoretical [British Marxist] tradition'.[23] Williams published his 'Notes' in *New Left Review* where in 1968 the editor Perry Anderson's seminal essay 'Components of the National Culture' had appeared.[24] On the same page where, in a footnote Williams, Hobsbawm and Christopher Hill are named by Anderson as 'individual exceptions', Anderson declares that 'the thirties [...] vaccinated British culture against Marxism. The fifties and sixties saw the proliferation of Marxism on the continent [...]. England remained unaffected. Marxist theory had never become naturalized'.[25] Anderson generalizes about the short-term radicalized intellectuals of the thirties that, firstly, because of 'political preoccupations'

18   Hans-Dieter Tschörtner, *49 Jahre internationale Literatur. Bibliographie 1947–1987* (Berlin: Volk und Welt, 1987), p. 386.

19   Jürgen Kuczinski [*sic*], 'Ein kritisches Wort über Buchbesprechungen', *Neues Deutschland*, 21 December 1946, p. 4.

20   Jürgen Kuczynski, 'Monopolisten und Junker – Todfeinde des deutschen Volkes' (Berlin-Prenzlauer Berg: *Tägliche Rundschau*, 1946).

21   Cem., 'Die Angst vor dem Geist', *Neues Deutschland*, 4 February 1948, p. 3.

22   N.A., 'Engels auf dem Scheiterhaufen. Radikaler Feldzug gegen demokratische Literatur', *Neues Deutschland*, 22 January 1948, p. 2.

23   Williams, *Notes on Marxism*, p. 90.

24   Perry Anderson, 'Components of the National Culture', *New Left Review*, 50, July/August 1968, 3–27.

25   Anderson, 'Components', p. 9.

they did not study 'Marx's own work', despite the fact that 'its genuine assimilation would have needed an immense work of theoretical study and reconversation', and that, secondly, 'their predominant occupations' 'facilitated' the 'persistence' of 'their inherited liberalism' 'often [...] quite unaltered [...] beneath their new political allegiance', because most were 'poets and natural scientists' – 'the two vocations most unsuited to effect any lasting political transformation of British culture'.[26]

In what follows I would like to make a case for Roy Pascal as a challenge to the – in my view – nationalistic assumption that Marxism, as something foreign, continental, un-British, was never naturalized in Britain. By taking as a point of departure the first few sentences of Pascal's foreword to Lukács's *Studies in European Realism,* I will attempt to prove Anderson's generalization wrong when he claimed: 'what the thirties so completely lacked – [was] a serious, scientific intellectual achievement'.[27]

Pascal wrote in 1950: 'This is I believe, the first book by Georg Lukács, the Hungarian Marxist, to be translated into English. Some of his studies have appeared in *International Literature,* and I have drawn attention to his work in three articles in *The Modern Quarterly* (for 1946, 1948 and 1949).' [28] As a first step, I will ask to which aspects of Lukács's work Pascal did in fact draw the attention of British readers and what kind of attention that was. The three articles in *The Modern Quarterly* and the foreword to *Studies in European Realism* will therefore be contextualized, not only, but primarily within the journal. As a second, briefer step I will discuss Pascal's publications prior to 1946 when he started to write about Lukács in the light of the question whether and how far Pascal was able to recognize his own scholarly work as a Marxist since 1933 in Lukács's essays. As a third and final step, I will look for lasting traces of Pascal's reception of Lukács in his work even after Pascal left the Communist Party of Great Britain (CPGB). The overall question running through all three steps – and, I hope, leading to an answer to the question posed in the title of this lecture – is whether Lukács's general thesis about the reception of revolutionary literature from one European country in another which at that time had no revolutionary literature of its own can be applied to Pascal's reception of Lukács. In 1945 Lukács wrote in *Studies in European Realism,*

> [...] that a really deep and serious impression cannot be made by any work of foreign literature unless there are [...] similar

---

26 Anderson, 'Components', p. 9.

27 Anderson, 'Components', p. 9.

28 Roy Pascal, 'Foreword', in Georg Lukács, *Studies in European Realism. A Sociological Survey of the Writings of Balzac, Stendhal, Zola, Tolstoy, Gorki and Others* (London: Hillway, 1950), pp. v-viii (p. v).

tendencies in existence – latently at least – in the country concerned. Such latency increases the fertility of foreign influences, for true influence is always the liberation of latent forces. It is precisely the rousing of latent energies that can make truly great foreign writers function as factors of a national literary development – unlike the superficial influences of passing fashions.[29]

Pascal's three articles on Lukács differ in genre: the first of 1946 is a 'simplified and elucidated' translated 'version'[30] of Lukács's essay 'On Prussiandom'[31] which had appeared in May 1943 in the Moscow-based journal *Internationale Literatur*; the second of 1948 is a review of Lukács's book *Goethe and His Time*,[32] first published in Hungary in 1946, a German version of which appeared one year later in Switzerland; and the third of 1949 is a 'synopsis' or 'summary' of the contribution of Lukács and (partly) the Austrian literary critic Ernst Fischer to the World Congress of Intellectuals for Peace, held in Wroclaw in August 1948.[33]

Pascal's 'rewriting'[34] of Lukács's 'On Prussiandom' into 'Prussianism and Nazism' not only cuts twenty pages down to eight, but concentrates the argument on the question in the title: 'Can we find any connection between the Prussian and the Nazi spirit?'.[35] Pascal uses the inclusive 'we' (though very rarely, actually only twice), but the answer given here is the transition from the first, shorter part (three pages) of the 'version' for 'British readers' to the longer one: 'Here a closer study is necessary of the Prussian, and remarkable insight into this problem is afforded by the evidence given by three of Germany's greatest writers, Heinrich von Kleist, Theodor Fontane, and Thomas Mann.'[36]

In the first part Pascal 'simplifies' Lukács's analysis of 'the peculiar course

---

29 Lukács, *Studies in European Realism*, p. 245.

30 Roy Pascal, 'Prussianism and Nazism', *The Modern Quarterly*, 1.3, Autumn 1946, 85–93 (p. 85).

31 Georg Lukács, 'Über Preußentum', in Georg Lukács, *Schicksalswende. Beiträge zu einer neuen deutschen Ideologie* (Berlin: Aufbau, 1948), pp. 68–95.

32 Georg Lukács, *Goethe und seine Zeit* (Budapest: Hungária, 1946 [1st edn.]).

33 Roy Pascal, 'Synopsis of the Contributions of Professor G. Lukács and Ernst Fischer to the Wroclaw Conference, 1948', *The Modern Quarterly*, 4.3, Summer 1949, 353–58 (p. 257). On this and the three following conferences in 1949, see Helmut Peitsch and Dirk Wiemann, 'Transformation of "Culture": From Anti-Fascism to Anti-Totalitarianism', *Comparative Critical Studies*, 13.2, 2016, 173–92.

34 Pascal, 'Prussianism and Nazism', p. 85.

35 Pascal, 'Prussianism and Nazism', p. 87.

36 Pascal, 'Prussianism and Nazism', p. 87.

of German history'[37] by cutting all detail, ordering the 'combination of [social-historical] elements' from which 'Prussianism arises'[38] into paragraphs on 'autocracy, Junkerdom, militarism, bureaucracy'[39] and giving a summary: 'Prussianism was the ideology of a people afraid of self-government, and finding a compensation in the glorification of power.'[40] In the second part, the analysis of Kleist's *The Prince of Homburg*, Fontane's *Schach von Wuthenow* and Mann's *Death in Venice*, Pascal 'follows [indeed] as closely as may be that of Lukács's version',[41] but by addressing his readers in the second person and by using the imperative Pascal brings to the fore his own elucidation:

> There is a remarkable consistency in the evidence on the Prussian character offered by these three writers [...]. Note that they are generally recognized to be in the first flight of German imaginative writers and are particularly distinguished for their insight into the human soul. Note, too, that all, when they wrote the works referred to above, were sympathetic to Prussia and Prussianism.[42]

However, what Pascal emphasizes as 'the greatness of the three authors', is 'that they recognized the contradictions and tensions within Prussianism',[43] and when, in the concluding paragraph, he stresses 'the tension between irrational individualism and authoritarianism' as 'an important aspect of the relationship between Prussianism and Nazism', he again uses the inclusive 'we': 'We see that in Prussianism there lie, suppressed, but always threatening to erupt, those forces of chaotic violence, lawlessness, brutality, which in Nazism come to the surface as a philosophy of society. [...]. It can be overcome only by the emergence of a true and radical democracy.'[44]

Pascal's final sentence hints at a context which may help explain what motivated him to rewrite an article published by Lukács three years before. On 2 February 1946, seven months before 'Prussianism and Nazism' appeared in *The Modern Quarterly*, Pascal attended a conference on 'Germany's Cultural Regeneration', organized by the British Council for German Democracy in London. Pascal's signature appears as a signatory under a message sent by the conference to Johannes R. Becher as President

37 Pascal, 'Prussianism and Nazism', p. 87.
38 Pascal, 'Prussianism and Nazism', p. 86.
39 Pascal, 'Prussianism and Nazism', p. 85.
40 Pascal, 'Prussianism and Nazism', p. 87.
41 Pascal, 'Prussianism and Nazism', p. 85.
42 Pascal, 'Prussianism and Nazism', p. 91.
43 Pascal, 'Prussianism and Nazism', p. 91.
44 Pascal, 'Prussianism and Nazism', p. 92.

of the Cultural League for Germany's Democratic Regeneration, expressing 'hope and belief that the evil doctrines of race hatred and militarism can be eradicated for ever'.[45] Among the other signatories were – apart from four Bishops, two Lords, twenty-five MPs and fifteen trade union leaders, the President of the English PEN Margaret Storm Jameson and the Secretary of the International PEN Hermon Ould, the General Secretary of UNESCO Julian Huxley, the writers Sean O'Casey and John Lehmann, the actors Laurence Olivier and Michael Redgrave and numerous professors.[46] They all 'promise[d]': 'We will support the Allied authorities in establishing closest co-operation with genuinely democratic elements and in the speedy and complete purging of Nazis and militarists from all educational and cultural institutions.'[47] At least Pascal, who had been Chairman of the Association of University Teachers (AUT) in 1944–45, fulfilled the promise: less than a year later, in January 1947, he was one of seven members of a 'delegation' of the AUT, invited by the Control Office of Germany and Austria to visit the universities in the British Zone to give advice on the commencement of relations between British and German universities.[48] The delegation's final report, for which Pascal was 'largely responsible',[49] calls for 'a break with the German tradition',[50] but concedes: 'The roots of all difficulties, however, lie very deep. The conservative, nationalistic, even reactionary attitude which one can observe in many German universities, reproduces

---

45   Alfred Meusel et al., *Germany's Cultural Regeneration. Conference of the British Council for German Democracy London, February 1946* (London: British Council for German Democracy, 1946). The document was reprinted, however, without the names of the signatories by Luise Dornemann, who provides some information on the 'particulary close relations' of the predecessor of the Council for German Democracy, the Allies Inside Germany Council, to British citizens in Birmingham (Luise Dornemann, 'Die Arbeit des Allies Inside Germany Council in Großbritannien (1942–1950)', *Beiträge zur Geschichte der Arbeiterbewegung*, 6, 1981, 872–91 (pp. 881 and 878). When the German translation of Pascal's *The Growth of Modern Germany* came out in the Soviet Zone of Occupation, it was prefaced by another participant at the Conference of the British Council for German Democracy in February 1946, Heinz Kamnitzer. He was then secretary to Alfred Meusel as the President of the Free German Institute of Science and Learning and keynote speaker at the conference. However, Pascal's book is completely ignored by Mario Keßler in his numerous articles on historians who returned from exile in Britain to East Germany; see for instance Mario Keßler, *Exilerfahrungen in Wissenschaft und Politik. Remigrierte Historiker in der frühen DDR* (Cologne: Böhlau, 2001).

46   Meusel, *Germany's Cultural Regeneration*, p. 11.

47   Meusel, *Germany's Cultural Regeneration*, p. 10.

48   N.A., 'Ausländische Berichte über deutsche Hochschulen II', *Hamburger Akademische Rundschau*, 2, 1947/48, 232–35 (p. 232).

49   Arrigo V. Subiotto, 'Roy Pascal, 1904–1980', *Proceedings of the British Academy*, 67, 1982, 442–57 (p. 449).

50   N.A., 'Ausländische Berichte', p. 232.

the social structure of the German people and the mentality of certain strata; it cannot be completely removed without changing this structure and this mentality'.[51] Therefore the report stresses that the delegation's proposals for reform 'do not exclusively or mainly aim at giving the German universities back their function as places of specialized research, but that the proposals are about replacing a limited German point of view by a European one in order to reintegrate German science and scholarship into the spiritual life of the European community'.[52] The report appeared in German translation in the student journals of two of the three universities Roy Pascal had visited with one half of the delegation: in the *Hamburger Akademische Rundschau* and the *Göttinger Universitäts-Zeitung* (not in the Kiel journal). In Göttingen, the report became part of a 'Debate about German Philology'[53] which took place in the student journal.

In the *Hamburger Akademische Rundschau*, however, Lukács's *Goethe and His Time* to which Roy Pascal drew the attention of British readers, was reviewed by a Hamburg student who regarded Lukács as 'not worthy of discussion'[54] and for whom his book was 'equally damnable as similar attempts from the Third Reich'.[55] Walter Boehlich called Lukács's linking of culture and politics 'rebarbarization',[56] as did another student, Horst Rüdiger: 'We experience the same politicization of scholarship which – under another sign – has already once confused the minds, but [now] with a sharper claim to totality.'[57] At the opening of his preface, Lukács sees a 'critical balancing'[58] as necessary because of the experience of Fascism and war, distancing it on the one hand from a 'global condemnation' of everything German, on the other from a 'global amnesty'[59] which 'amounts

---

51 N.A., 'Ausländische Berichte', p. 233.

52 N.A., 'Ausländische Berichte', p. 234.

53 Pier Carlo Bontempelli, 'Die Rolle der *Göttinger Universitäts-Zeitung* und der *Hamburger Akademischen Rundschau* in der Erneuerung der Universität, im literarischen Leben und im Selbstverständnis der deutschen Literaturwissenschaft der ersten Nachkriegsjahre', *Igitur*, 7.2, 1995, 57–71 (p. 63).

54 Walter Boehlich, 'Georg Lukács: *Goethe und seine Zeit'*, *Hamburger Akademische Rundschau*, 3, 1948–50, 700–03 (p. 700).

55 Boehlich, 'Georg Lukács', p. 703.

56 Boehlich, 'Georg Lukács', p. 700.

57 Horst Rüdiger, 'Der "progressive Goethe". Zu Georg Lukacs' *Goethe und seine Zeit'*, *Der Standpunkt*, 3.10, 1949, p. 9.

58 Georg Lukács, 'Goethe und seine Zeit. Vorwort', in G. Lukács, *Faust und Faustus. Vom Drama der Menschengattung zur Tragödie der modernen Kunst* (Berne: Francke, 1947 [1st edn.]; Reinbek: Rowohlt, 1967), pp. 7–16 (p. 7).

59 Lukács, 'Goethe', p. 10.

to a separation of the phenomena from the social ground on which they have grown'.[60] The historically concrete 'critical balancing' of progressive and reactionary tendencies in German cultural development implies 'that the progressive tendencies are the allies of any tendency to the renewal of Europe' abroad .[61] Thus for Lukács the two 'decisive questions' which have been wrongly answered by German Germanistik's 'history of the [German] spirit' are, firstly, the 'relation [of German literature] to the world movement of the enlightenment', and secondly, the 'alleged opposition of the Sturm und Drang to the enlightenment'.[62]

Whereas Lukács expressly rejects the assumption of the 'general amnesty', namely 'that the political development of the last decades should not influence our philosophical and literary judgments in any respect,[63] Boehlich explicitly affirms this maxim: 'To stand by the Literature of the Time of Goethe does not mean to approve the German development of the twentieth century.'[64] But Boehlich goes further when he excludes not only Marxism, but also its historical sources from German culture: 'Lukács looks for things in Germany which have not existed in Germany, because he walks in the tracks of Marxism for which surely the social revolution of France and the industrial revolution of England have become decisive. Instead of both, Germany has experienced a literary revolution, the revolution of the Time of Goethe'.[65]

However, the majority of reviews which, following on from Roy Pascal's relatively early one in *The Modern Quarterly* in 1948, were published by German exiles in the USA and Sweden as well as by French and British Germanists, agreed on the importance of Lukács's critique of the anti-western, anti-enlightenment construction of German literary history of the late eighteenth and early nineteenth centuries as a 'German Movement'.[66] Herbert Marcuse wrote: 'One of the finest achievements of Lukács's book is his successful fight against the irrationalistic-metaphysical interpretation of classical German literature (especially Dilthey and Gundolf).'[67] In

60   Lukács, 'Goethe', p. 7.

61   Lukács, 'Goethe', p. 8.

62   Lukács, 'Goethe', p. 13.

63   Lukács, 'Goethe', p. 7.

64   Boehlich, 'Georg Lukács', p. 703.

65   Boehlich, 'Georg Lukács', p. 703.

66   Helmut Peitsch, '"The wind from the east is cold – but invigorating". Die Rezeption von Georg Lukács' *Goethe und seine Zeit* in den Westzonen Deutschlands', *Goethe Jahrbuch*, 103, 1986, 200–06.

67   Herbert Marcuse, '*Goethe und seine Zeit*. Georg Lukács (1947)', *Philosophy and Phenomenology Research*, 9.1, 1950, 142–44 (p. 143).

this context, Roy Pascal's review stands out because it does not focus on Germany's special path; he attributes 'utmost importance' to Lukács's book as 'rescuing [*sic*] [... Goethe] for the forward movement of humanity of which he felt himself a part'.[68] Pascal therefore does not discuss the two essays on Schiller and Hölderlin, but concentrates firmly on Goethe and only three of the works Lukács deals with – *Werther*, *Wilhelm Meister* and *Faust*. Including his British readers in the first-person plural 'we' form, Pascal writes about the way his review will present the findings of Lukács on Goethe: 'We see in him a succession of interpretations [of the world], developing as he grows and reflecting the great events through which he lived. [...] He [...] stimulates in us a heightened perception of our own times. He can himself be understood only as a dynamic, evolutionary process.'[69] Pascal's identification of Goethe with humanity is recognizable in his conclusion: 'We cannot only win from him a deeper understanding of the human process, but gain from him inspiration boldly to seek the realisation of the potentialities of man in modern conditions.'[70] The only time that Pascal implicitly refers to Lukács's preface is when he introduces the guiding aspect for his presentation of Goethe's works: 'As Heine pointed out and Marx stressed, Germany took part theoretically in the revolution England and France fought out practically, and Goethe, like Hegel, was able to comprehend and express the character of this revolution more fully than those actually engaged in it.'[71] Thus in *Werther* 'the central demand [of the young European bourgeoisie] for untrammelled development of all potentialities of man',[72] 'is necessarily frustrated by the nature of civil society';[73] *Wilhelm Meister*, termed by Lukács 'an education towards reality', 'condemns the prose [of bourgeois society], but also condemns the blind revolt against it'.[74] And 'the whole process of Faust's development – and by Faust he means explicitly mankind – is good, despite its violence and destructiveness'.[75]

In the same issue of *The Modern Quarterly* in which Roy Pascal's third article appeared drawing attention to Lukács, John D. Bernal gave a report of the Wroclaw World Congress of Intellectuals for Peace. Bernal concedes that

68 Roy Pascal, '*Goethe und Seine* [*sic*] *Zeit*. By Georg Lukács', *The Modern Quarterly*, 4.1, 1948/49, 76–83 (p. 76).

69 Pascal, '*Goethe und Seine* [*sic*] *Zeit*', p. 77.

70 Pascal, '*Goethe und Seine* [*sic*] *Zeit*', p. 82.

71 Pascal, '*Goethe und Seine* [*sic*] *Zeit*', p. 77.

72 Pascal, '*Goethe und Seine* [*sic*] *Zeit*', p. 77.

73 Pascal, '*Goethe und Seine* [*sic*] *Zeit*', p. 78.

74 Pascal, '*Goethe und Seine* [*sic*] *Zeit*', p. 79.

75 Pascal, '*Goethe und Seine* [*sic*] *Zeit*', p. 81.

his 'analysis'[76] of the 'world as it is to-day',[77] based on the speeches he heard in Wroclaw, 'will [...] not be acceptable, even comprehensible, to the great majority of intellectuals in this country'.[78] The most quoted statement on Wroclaw in the British mainstream press was that of historian A.J.P. Taylor to *The Times* of 26 August 1948: 'that he stood for the unity of all mankind, but if that could not be obtained, then he was for the common European tradition of intellectual liberty, more than one way of being right, freedom of mind, and the artist's freedom of creation'. 'Unless we can meet on that basis, we can meet on none', he said. This setting of Europe as Western cultural freedom against the USSR, the People's Democracies of eastern Europe and the colonies as denominating a lack of this culture had been an issue of discussion in Wroclaw. Bernal quotes Ilya Ehrenburg who stated: 'We do not divide human culture into zones according to latitude or longitude, but we know that history moves.'[79] Ehrenburg asked:

Can [...Western culture] be opposed to Russian as being a different culture, i.e. 'Eastern'. Historically, this is absurd [...]. I must ask the apologists of 'Western culture' what the literature of France, England and the United States would have looked like if the classic Russian novel had not appeared on the world stage in the latter half of the nineteenth century, if there had been no Tolstoy and Dostoyevsky, Turgenyev and Tchekov.[80]

One answer to this question is given in Lukács's *Studies in European Realism* and its foreword by Roy Pascal. From the minutes of the Congress, published in French in Warsaw in 1949,[81] it becomes clear that Lukács, in an afternoon session, took up the point made by Ehrenburg in the morning:

The modern western European literature from Bernard Shaw to [Roger Martin] du Gard, from Romain Rolland to Thomas Mann would be unthinkable without Tolstoi. Every expert on literature knows that the reception of Shakespeare in France has been much more difficult than the one of Tolstoi in western Europe',[82] 'but

76 J.D. Bernal, 'Wroclaw and After', *The Modern Quarterly*, 4.1, 1948/49, 5–27 (p. 25).
77 Bernal, 'Wroclaw', p. 20.
78 Bernal, 'Wroclaw', p. 25.
79 Bernal, 'Wroclaw', p. 10.
80 Bernal, 'Wroclaw', p. 12.
81 'Discours de M. György Lukacs' [*sic*], in *Congrès mondial des intellectuels pour la paix in Wroclaw-Pologne 25–28 août 1948. Compte-rendu présenté par le bureau du secrétaire général* (Warsaw: Prasa, 1949), pp. 79–84 (p. 82).
82 Georg Lukács, 'Verantwortlichkeit der Intellektuellen', in *Der Weltfriedenskongress*

[the apologists of 'Western culture'...] do not build a Chinese Wall of separation between the culture of France and England.[83]

In his foreword to Lukács's *Studies in European Realism*, Roy Pascal uses the image of the 'iron curtain' seemingly only in passing, however, it is in a programmatical formulation on 'Marxist [literary] criticism': 'Just as it will tolerate no iron curtain between spirit and matter, between individual and society, so it sees the past living in the present'.[84] It 'shows how great literature crystallizes attitudes, intensifies our consciousness of the world in which we live, and rallies us to participate more fully in this world'.[85] These characteristics relate to Marxist literary criticism in general: 'This is the significance of [Christopher] Caudwell's work in England [...] and of the recent discussions in the Soviet Union.'[86] Pascal stresses: 'His Marxism has enabled Lukács to come to true literary criticism, that is the analysis of literary forms and their development in terms of the reality [...] of particular times, of the changes in society and the subjective experience of the writer.'[87] Pascal describes *Studies in European Realism* as a 'blending of literary criticism, philosophical and psychological analysis, and sociological grasp'.[88] He emphasizes as Lukàcs's 'most stimulating approach' the fact that his 'Marxism does not dissolve aesthetics into sociology, but gives a key to understanding of aesthetic problems', namely 'form and content', 'realism and its relationship to naturalism and romanticism', 'the particular and the type', 'the conscious intention of the creative writer and his actual achievement'. Pascal summarizes these problems as one: 'the problem of objective aesthetic judgments'.[89] Equally this term is used when Pascal describes the objects of Lukács's *Studies in European Realism*: for Pascal, Lukács's reading of Balzac, Stendhal, Belinsky, Dobrolyubov, Chernyshevksy and Tolstoy does not only 'show the unity of this great humanistic tradition of protest against capitalism'[90] against its 'violent distortion of human

der Kulturschaffenden. Ein Material für Referenten (Berlin: Kulturbund zur demokratischen Erneuerung Deutschlands, 1948), pp. 26–30 (p. 29).

83   Georg Lukács, 'Von der Verantwortung der Intellektuellen (1948)', in N.A., *Georg Lukács, zum siebzigsten Geburtstag* (Berlin: Aufbau, 1955), pp. 232–42 (p. 240).

84   Pascal, 'Foreword', p. vii.

85   Pascal, 'Foreword', p. vii.

86   Pascal, 'Foreword', p. vii.

87   Pascal, 'Foreword', p. vi.

88   Pascal, 'Foreword', p. vi.

89   Pascal, 'Foreword', p. vii.

90   Pascal, 'Foreword', p. vi.

life',[91] but also 'formulate[s], on the basis of their relationship to humanity, principles of objective aesthetic judgments'.[92] This degree of identification distinguishes Roy Pascal from other British Marxist literary critics. His allusion to Caudwell and the discussions in the Soviet Union in the foreword mark the field in which other British Marxist critics positioned themselves by reviewing *Studies in European Realism*.[93]

In the same issue of *The Modern Quarterly* in which Arnold Kettle's review of Lukács's *Studies in European Realism* appeared, Maurice Cornforth opened what was to become 'The Caudwell Discussion' by stating: 'British Marxists will never come near a Marxist approach to art, let alone work out a comprehensive theory of it, until they [...] reject all those false premises and idealist notions which put Caudwell off the track.'[94] In the early 1950s, however, Roy Pascal at least succeeded in drawing the attention of British Marxist literary critics to Lukács's conception of European Realism as characterized by 'the human and artistic identification of the writer with some broad popular movement' 'struggling for the emancipation of the common people'.[95] Although *Studies in European Realism* only covers French and Russian literature, the two essays 'The International Significance of Russian Democratic Criticism' and 'Leo Tolstoy and Western European

---

91   Pascal, 'Foreword', pp. vi-vii.

92   Pascal, 'Foreword', p. vii.

93   Although Pascal was included in Lee Baxandall's 1968 *Selective Annotated Bibliography* on Marxism and Aesthetics in English (with twelve items), he was absent from Chris Bullock's and David Peck's 1980 *Guide to Marxist Literary Criticism* in English and from Victor N. *Paananen's 2000 British Marxist Criticism* which covers (apart from critics mentioned in this lecture, i.e. Christopher Caudwell, Jack Lindsay and Alick West) only A.L. Morton, Margot Heinemann, Raymond Williams and Terry Eagleton. In Edwin A. Roberts's *The Anglo-Marxists* Lukács is only mentioned once as the (by 'Anglo-Marxists' ignored) author of *History and Class Consciousness* because Roberts follows Perry Anderson's concept of the traditional British national culture of liberalism and empiricism (Edwin A. Roberts, *The Anglo-Marxists: A Study in Ideology and Culture* (Lanham, MD: Rowman & Littlefield, 1997), p. 3). In his *International Bibliography* on Lukács François H. Lapointe calls Pascal's introduction '[n]ot worth consulting' (François H. Lapointe, *Georg Lukács and His Critics. An International Biography with Annotations, 1910–1982* (Westport, CO: Greenwood Press, 1983), p. 205). However, he neither identifies the article by Lukács to which Pascal's 'Prussianism and Nazism' refers nor lists Pascal's review of *Goethe and His Time*.

94   Maurice Cornforth, 'Caudwell and Marxism', *The Modern Quarterly*, 6.1, 1950/51, 16–33 (p. 26).

95   Lukács, *Studies in European Realism*, p. 18. For George Lichtheim it was exactly 'the construction of a "bourgeois-revolutionary" background to sustain the myth of a great popular tradition of progressivism' which as a 'political purpose' disqualified Lukács's literary criticism and excluded it not only from scholarship, but from European culture (George Lichtheim, 'An Intellectual Disaster', *Encounter*, 20, May 1963, 74–80 (p. 96)).

Literature' demonstrate not only that the Russian realists were the 'heirs' of the French,[96] but that also for English and German literature revolutionary democracy was 'the bridge between the old and new culture,[97] because '[f] rom the French revolution onwards the development of society' in Europe 'on the one hand gave birth to the ideal of the complete human personality and on the other hand destroyed it in practice'.[98] In his contribution to the Geneva conference on the 'European Spirit' in 1946, Lukács explained this contradiction:

> The crises of democracy, of the idea of progress, of the belief in rationality and of humanism originate from the victory of the Great French Revolution [...] because this victory brought out the developed contradictions of capitalism. The ideological consequence was that the emerging social state contains a fulfillment and a refutation of the ideas of the Enlightenment at the same time and in an inseparable way.[99]

It is in these European crises that, for Lukács, one's own national humanist and democratic tendencies can be liberated by the European Other: 'Where decay is greatest, there the desire for regeneration is the strongest.'[100] Lukács states in the preface: 'It was thus that Goethe aided Walter Scott, and Walter Scott aided Balzac.'[101]

---

96 Lukács, *Studies in European Realism*, p. 5.

97 Lukács, *Studies in European Realism*, p. 16.

98 Lukács, *Studies in European Realism*, p. 13.

99 Lukács, *Studies in European Realism*, p. 199. This view was misrepresented by Maurice Merleau-Ponty in the only reference to Lukács in *Humanism and Terror* (1947) in the following way: in Geneva Lukács 'started with the classical critique of the formal democracy in order finally to ask the intellectuals of the West to uphold again exactly those democratic ideas he had just claimed to be dead' (Maurice Merleau-Ponty, *Humanismus und Terror* (Frankfurt/M: Hain, 1990), p. 21). See his own Geneva contribution which makes the same point: M. Merleau-Ponty, 'Crisis in European Consciousness' [1946] in M. Merleau-Ponty, *Texts and Dialogues. On Philosophy, Politics, and Culture*, ed. by Hugh J. Silverman and James Barry Jr. (Atlantic Highlands, NJ: Humanities Press, 1992), pp. 17–18.

100 Lukács, *Studies in European Realism*, p. 246.

101 Lukács, *Studies in European Realism*, p. 19. By not referring to the so-called 'theory of Social Fascism' of the Communist International, Pascal's book differs from the chapter on Germany in *Fascism and Social Revolution. A Study of the Economics and Politics of the Extreme Stages of Capitalism in Decay*, which Rajani Palme Dutt, founder and member of the Executive Committee of the CPGB, published in the same year (London: Lawrence, 1934).

Three Marxist critics, Arnold Kettle, Jack Lindsay and Alick West, initially accepted the official critique of Lukács by the Hungarian Workers' Party in particular for – as Hobsbawm approvingly summarized – 'softening the sharp outline of the break between the old and the new, indeed for losing sight of the advance to socialism in his eagerness to maintain continuity with the past'.[102] However, these critics changed their position in the early 1950s when publishing in the three journals of the CPGB – *The Modern Quarterly, Communist Review* and *Labour Monthly* – and contributing to three conferences on culture, organized by the Party between 1950 and 1952.[103]

In his review of Lukács's *Studies in European Realism*, Arnold Kettle twice emphasizes a 'link' to a British Marxist critic. On 1848 as a turning point in European literary history Kettle writes: 'Lukács, like [Ralph] Fox, sees Flaubert's work as the beginning of the disintegration'[104] 'of the realist tradition of Western Europe' whereas it 'continued to grow [...] in Russia'.[105] With regard to '[t]he theory of typicality' which 'seems' to Kettle 'to be Lukács' most original and most important contribution to a Marxist literary criticism',[106] he asks: 'Is there not here, in the emphasis on the concrete nature of art [...] a note which echoes [Christopher] Caudwell [...]?'.[107] In his conference contribution on 'The Progressive Tradition in Bourgeois Culture' he names first Shakespeare and Milton, but then brackets them together with Goethe, Heine, Balzac and Tolstoy,[108] emphasizing their 'values of humanity'[109] and adds that 'bourgeois realism in general' was 'highly critical [...] of bourgeois society'.[110]

The writer and critic Jack Lindsay, who in 1937 in the Left Review had reviewed Fox's *The Novel and the People* as 'outstanding', and 'as one of the main contributions to the English foundation of Marxism',[111] ascribed

102   Eric Hobsbawm, 'Introduction', in Josef Révai: *Lukács & Socialism Realism. A Hungarian Literary Controversy*. (London: Fore Publications, 1950), pp. i-iv (p. ii).

103   Cf. Alick West, 'A Critic of Literature. Review of Georg Lukács, *Studies in European Realism', Labour Monthly*, 33.2, February 1951, 92–93; and Alick West, 'Review of Josef Revai, Lukács and Socialist Realism', *Labour Monthly*, 34.6, June 1952, p. 288.

104   Arnold Kettle, 'Review of Georg Lukács, *Studies in European Realism', The Modern Quarterly*, 6.1, 1950/51, 72–81 (p. 73).

105   Kettle, 'Review', p. 74.

106   Kettle, 'Review', p. 79.

107   Kettle, 'Review', p. 80.

108   Arnold Kettle, 'The Progressive Tradition in Bourgeois Culture', in *Essays on Socialist Realism and the British Cultural Tradition* (London: Arena Publications, n.d.), pp. 32–42 (p. 32).

109   Kettle, 'The Progressive Tradition', p. 35.

110   Kettle, 'The Progressive Tradition', p. 36.

111   Jack Lindsay, 'Marxism and the Novel', *Left Review*, 3.1, February 1937, 51–53 (p. 52).

'a special significance and importance' within 'all that is valuable' to that 'which is largely rooted in problems still directly affecting us'.[112] Lindsay relates 'the progressive tradition of our 19th century writers' to the 'great mass-movements of the 1830s and 1840s [...] rising up out of our people and deeply affecting our national culture': 'Consider their entire partisanship of the liberation movements of Europe.'[113]

Alick West, in his contribution to the conference 'Socialist Realism and the British Cultural Tradition' maintains:

> Between the heroes of the past histories of all countries – we have our Shakespeare, France has her Rabelais, Spain her Cervantes, Germany her Goethe, Russia her Puschkin – and between the nameless millions who made their greatness possible, there is a comradeship of common endeavour. All of them [...] were fighting for man's freedom and progress. That is the content of our national tradition, as it is the tradition of all nations.[114]

This 'content of our patriotism',[115] which is 'carrying the bourgeois democratic revolution forward into the socialist revolution',[116] West calls 'humanism'.[117] In an article on T.S. Eliot, West emphasizes that for Eliot 'literature of Europe [...] means, in fact, of western Europe'[118] and a 'glorification of the culture of the past, especially of hierarchic feudalism'[119] by praising Burke who 'out of English tradition [...] tried to make chains for the English people, so that they should feel themselves, not the citizens

---

112 Jack Lindsay, 'The Progressive Tradition of Our 19ᵗʰ-Century Writers', in *Britain's Cultural Heritage: Symposium, London, May 25, 1951* (London: Arena Publications, 1951), pp. 43–45 (p. 43).

113 Lindsay, 'The Progressive Tradition', p. 43. When Lindsay met Lukács (and Ernst Fischer) at the conferences of Wroclaw and Paris in 1948 and 1949, he remembers in a later reworking of two articles from 1964 and 1973, that he had only read Lukács's essay on Walter Scott published in the English version of 'International Literature' (Jack Lindsay, 'The Part and the Whole: The Achievement of Georg Lukács', in *Decay and Renewal. Critical Essays on Twentieth-Century Writers* (London: Lawrence and Wishart, 1976), pp. 11–51 (p. 50)). Lindsay's article, however, contains a close reading of two of the essays in *Studies in European Realism*, namely the first ones on Balzac's *The Peasants* and *Lost Illusions*.

114 Alick West, 'The British Road to Socialism', in *Essays on Socialist Realism and the British Cultural Tradition*, ed. by Jack Lindsay (London: Arena, n.d.), pp. 78–86 (p. 79).

115 West, 'The British Road', p. 80.

116 West, 'The British Road', p. 79.

117 West, 'The British Road', p. 80.

118 Alick West, 'The Abuse of Poetry and the Abuse of Criticism by T.S. Eliot', *Marxist Quarterly*, January 1954, 22–32, (p. 24).

119 West, 'The Abuse of Poetry', p. 25.

of a democracy, but the humble subjects of a State majestic with all the authority of the past'[120] and by speaking of 'the bourgeois revolution [...] as the Civil War'.[121] West appeals to his readers: 'Compare with Gorky's, Plekhanow's, Mehring's and Lukács's revolution in literary criticism the concepts underlying Eliot's "Tradition and the Individual Talent".'[122]

Having attempted as the first step in my argument to demonstrate that Pascal's articles on Lukács in *The Modern Quarterly* and his foreword to the first English-language edition of essays by Lukács achieved a receptive attention for Lukács's socio-historical humanist concept of literary criticism – at least among British Marxist literary critics such as Arnold Kettle, Jack Lindsay and Alick West – I would like to ask how this success can be explained. Pascal's appropriation of Lukács's concept was based on the possibility that Pascal could recognize his own Marxist work after 1933 in Lukács's writings, when he started to read them. There is no reference to Lukács in any book or article Pascal published prior to his English version of Lukács's 'On Prussiandom' of 1946. But – contrary to Perry Anderson's generalization about British Communists of the 1930s – Pascal did read Marx's works, and he had the advantage of being a Germanist which meant that he could also include those not yet published in English. When, in 1939, Pascal edited the first English translation of Marx's and Engels's *The German Ideology*, leaving out the second part on Bruno Bauer, he based it on the Moscow 'Marx Engels Complete Edition' (MEGA). In the preface he uses two triads to describe on the one hand 'the first full statement of Marxism',[123] and on the other, its present 'value'.[124] The first triad characterizes *The German Ideology* as Marx's and Engels's 'view of the relationship between the economic, political and intellectual activities of man';[125] the second refers to 'the development of human society which is essentially a history of "material production" through the division of labour, i.e., of the growth of private property'; the third to 'the relations between economic forces and political, juridical, theoretical forms' as 'an outline of human relations in communist society'.[126] The way that the term 'relationship' in the first formulation returns in the second to again connect economy, politics and intellectual activity, corresponds to the

---

120 West, 'The Abuse of Poetry', p. 25.

121 West, 'The Abuse of Poetry', p. 26.

122 West, 'The Abuse of Poetry', p. 24.

123 Roy Pascal, 'Introduction', in Karl Marx, Friedrich Engels, *The German Ideology. Part 1 and 3*, ed. by Roy Pascal (New York: International Publishers, 1939), pp. ix-xviii (p. xi).

124 Pascal, 'Introduction', p. xvi.

125 Pascal, 'Introduction', p. ix.

126 Pascal, 'Introduction', p. xvi.

interest Pascal had by 1939 demonstrated in the role of the division of labour in history and in ideology as an expression of class interest. Remarkable is the correspondence, suggested by the triads, between 'intellectual activity' and 'human relations in communist society'. There is, however, a difference between Pascal's first books and articles and the ones which followed his working through of all the early writings of Marx published in the MEGA under the over-arching question: How did Marx become a Marxist?

Both Pascal's books published in 1933–34, namely *The Social Basis of the German Reformation: Martin Luther and his Times* and *The Nazi Dictatorship*, are examples of historical materialism as 'class-struggle analysis'.[127] The key thesis of Pascal's book on Luther is that 'the consistency of the contradictions' of Luther's theology[128] and of his 'thought and activity in other spheres'[129] 'is the consistency of class interest'.[130] He accordingly assesses the 'Nazi Dictatorship' in 1934 as follows: 'The main force in Germany to-day is Monopoly-Capitalism. Its policy is war. […] All institutions through which their working-class opponents may work have been destroyed'.[131] This analysis, however, does not prevent Pascal from taking Nazi anti-Semitism very seriously, even if in class terms: 'The possibility of a pogrom in the Czarist fashion lies in the sphere of practical politics.'[132]

Pascal's article on the 'Scottish Historical School'[133] and the anthology *Shakespeare in Germany 1740–1815*[134] follow the trail from *The German Ideology* to one of the three theoretical sources of Marxism, namely, British Political Economy of the eighteenth century, which in 1913 Lenin in *The Three Sources and Three Component Parts of Marxism*[135] distinguished from the other two, French Utopian Socialism and German Classical Philosophy. In his reading of Adam Smith, Adam Ferguson, John Millar and William Robertson, Pascal on the one hand points out their common 'main theme, that "civil society"

127 Harvey J. Kaye, *The British Marxist Historians. An Introductory Analysis* (London: Macmillan, 1995 [1st edn. 1984]), p. 5.

128 Roy Pascal, *The Social Basis of the German Reformation. Martin Luther and his Times* (London: Watts & Co, 1933), p. 227.

129 Pascal, *The Social Basis*, p. 226.

130 Pascal, *The Social Basis*, p. 227.

131 Roy Pascal, *The Nazi Dictatorship* (London: Routledge, 1934), pp. 268–69.

132 Pascal, *The Nazi Dictatorship*, pp. 145–46.

133 Roy Pascal, 'Herder and the Scottish Historical School', *Publications of the English Goethe Society*, n.s. 14, 1939, 23–42.

134 Roy Pascal, *Shakespeare in Germany 1740–1815* (Cambridge: Cambridge University Press, 1937).

135 V.I. Lenin, *The Three Sources and Three Component Parts of Marxism*, in V.I. Lenin, *Collected Works*, vol. 19 (Moscow: Progress Publishers, 1977), pp. 21–28.

owes its form and development to the structure and development of private property, and that the mode of this social development is one of progress through internal contradictions, through the struggle between classes with an antagonistic relationship to property',[136] and on the other – following Marx –, he prefers Ferguson who 'emphasizes much more than Smith the harmful effects of the division of labour', for instance on 'the public spirit of earlier forms of society' (which Ferguson tends to idealise), and acknowledges that 'property produces "civil antagonisms"',[137] whereas Smith's 'outline of modern society does not even mention the English revolution [...] wilfully avoiding the political forms the class-struggle took'.[138]

Pascal's writings on Shakespeare and the Scottish historians reflected his interest in their German reception in the past and in the present within the 'framework of the rise of capitalism all over Europe'. Thus the introduction to *Shakespeare in Germany 1740–1815* opens with the rebuttal of Friedrich Gundolf's 'German Spirit', which Pascal roundly rejects as a 'misconception',[139] because 'the attitude to Shakespeare in this period is [...] part of a changing moral and social outlook' and the selected texts 'suggest the connections between aesthetic, moral and social principles raised by the writings of Shakespeare'.[140] In 'Herder and the Scottish Historical School' Pascal focuses on Ferguson and elaborates the critique of Friedrich Meinecke's 1936 concept of historicism which he formulated in the first article about the School itself: 'Meinecke [...] distorts Ferguson's thought by saying that he sees the decisive cause of the rise or decay of peoples in their spiritual attitude towards the State [Staatsgesinnung] – a conclusion convenient for present-day Germany.'[141] By focusing his detailed comparison of Ferguson and Herder on the two terms which for Meinecke make up the 'main characteristics' of his concept of (a specifically German) historicism: 'uniqueness' [Eigenwert] [...] and 'development' [Entwicklung][142] Pascal proves that Meinecke turns Herder's lack of a 'clearer grasp' into an 'achievement'[143]: '[b]y postulating a lack of change in each people [...Herder] comes to an over-emphatic definition of its specific characteristics; and,

---

136   Roy Pascal, 'Property and Society. The Scottish Historical School of the Eighteenth Century', *The Modern Quarterly*, 1.1, 1938, 167–79 (p. 178).

137   Pascal, 'Property and Society', p. 173.

138   Pascal, 'Property and Society', p. 179.

139   Pascal, *Shakespeare in Germany*, p. 1.

140   Pascal, 'Foreword' in Pascal, *Shakespeare in Germany*, pp. ix-x (p. ix).

141   Pascal, 'Property and Society', p. 178.

142   Pascal, 'Introduction', in *The German Ideology*, by Karl Marx and Friedrich Engels, p. 26.

143   Pascal, 'Introduction', in *The German Ideology*, p. 40.

similarly, the process of historical development takes on a transcendental, mysterious garb.'[144]

In 1942 and 1943, when Pascal published two essays on Marx, thereby marking the centenary of the initial publication of Marx's writings, he participated in 'a series of Discussion Meetings on the German 'Mind and Outlook' organised by the Institute of Sociology, London.[145] Like the other participants' papers, Pascal's on 'Nationalism and the German Intellectuals' appeared only in 1945, with a challenging sentence in the first paragraph: 'Nothing is more untrue than that the Germans "have always been the same"'.[146] As far as the economic, social and political conditions of Fascism are concerned, Pascal develops the main thesis of *The Growth of Modern Germany* and arrives at the same conclusion[147] as in the paper of the German 'Mind and Outlook' series: 'two real factors [...] which apply in all [imperialist] countries [...] constitute a threat to democracy everywhere',[148] 'a class society' and an 'international system' with 'foreign possessions'. 'Only the elimination of these two factors can provide a guarantee that German nationalism in its terrible modern form will cease to exist.'[149] For the 'specific conditions' why 'nationalistic imperialism [...] found in Germany its sharpest and most barbaric form',[150] Pascal refers to 1848 as 'a turning-point'[151] when 'the contradiction between democracy and nationalism began to reveal itself in Germany'.[152] Then Nationalism turned from 'one of

---

144   Pascal, 'Introduction', in *The German Ideology*, pp. 40–1.

145   Wolfgang Brenn has drawn attention to Pascal's *The Nazi Dictatorship* in his article 'British "Germanistik" and the Problem of National Socialism', *German Life and Letters*, 42, 1989, 145–67 (p. 161): 'It is most untypical in its unwavering Marxist approach and in its sovereign transgression of the boundaries of the university discipline.' However, he does not mention Pascal's contribution to 'Mind and Outlook' which he calls 'of lesser interest' since he mistakes Pascal's and others' critique of Prussianism as a 'compromise [...] sometimes supported by Socialists' (p. 163) between the conservative 'one Germany' and the liberal 'two Germanies' concepts.

146   Roy Pascal, 'Nationalism and the German Intellectuals', in G.P. Gooch, Morris Ginsberg, L.A. Willoughby, E.M. Butler, S.D. Stirk, Roy Pascal, *The German Mind and Outlook. With a Summary by Alexander Farquharson. Issued under the Auspices of the Institute of Sociology* (London: Chapman & Hall, 1945), pp. 160–90 (p. 160).

147   Pascal, *Deutschland ⭢ Weg und Irrweg*, p. 173.

148   Pascal, 'Nationalism and the German Intellectuals', p. 189.

149   Pascal, 'Nationalism and the German Intellectuals', p. 190.

150   Pascal, *Deutschland – Weg und Irrweg*, p. 173.

151   Pascal, 'Nationalism and the German Intellectuals', p. 170.

152   Pascal, 'Nationalism and the German Intellectuals', pp. 171–2.

defence' to 'one of [aggression],[153] power and conquest'.[154] Since the 'belated foundation [of the Reich], dominated by militaristic Prussia'[155] and 'so much later than other nations',[156] this turn of German nationalism made the SPD 'in its internationalism […] a threat to German expansion'[157]: 'in the conflict between imperialisms and the struggle between classes, lie, I believe, the sources of the violent nationalism which' 'gave to German nationalism its specific, extravagant and ruthless character' and 'even then [1848] slipped over into racialism'.[158] Pascal focuses on three intellectual contributors to the development of German nationalism into Fascism, Treitschke, Nietzsche and Spengler, but it is his critique of Nietzsche that comes closest to the reason for his interest in Lukács's humanist, revolutionary-democratic European Realism:

> Nietzsche was no narrow nationalist. But more than any contemporary does he strike at the roots of rational humanism, of internationalism, of democracy. Nietzsche does not set out from nationalism. He prides himself in being a 'good European'. His starting-point is hatred of democracy, of all movements which assert that classes or nations have equal rights […]. He aimed at the heart of the democratic, humanistic way of thinking. […] he led the onslaught on reason which has culminated in the Nazi ideology.[159]

In his two-part account of '[t]he development of Marx's outlook',[160] firstly 'His Apprenticeship to Politics', and secondly 'Political Foundations', Pascal repeatedly refers to its social and historical conditions: 'The economic backwardness and political fragmentation of Germany delayed development of the bourgeois class as a whole; but bourgeois intellectuals, in direct contact with events and thought in the advanced capitalist countries, revolutionised traditional modes of thinking.'[161] However, another emphasis is apparent when Pascal suggests to his readers a particular way of reading Marx: 'The

---

153 Pascal, 'Nationalism and the German Intellectuals', p. 173.

154 Pascal, 'Nationalism and the German Intellectuals', p. 172.

155 Pascal, 'Nationalism and the German Intellectuals', p. 174.

156 Pascal, 'Nationalism and the German Intellectuals', p. 173.

157 Pascal, 'Nationalism and the German Intellectuals', p. 174.

158 Pascal, 'Nationalism and the German Intellectuals', p. 174.

159 Pascal, 'Nationalism and the German Intellectuals', pp. 180–1.

160 Roy Pascal, 'Karl Marx. His Apprenticeship to Politics' (London: Labour Monthly, 1942).

161 Pascal, 'Karl Marx. His Apprenticeship', p. 5.

student is still gripped by the power and tenacity of Marx's thought, his vitality and wit, by the integrity and moral passion of his character.'[162] The humanist understanding of Marxism at which the introduction to the English edition of The German Ideology hinted is worked out more fully in the two biographical essays. In Pascal's careful textual analysis of Marx's writings, the reader's attention is drawn piece by piece primarily to Marx's 'determination to establish a society over which man has domination – a "human society or social humanity" as he calls it in the "Theses on Feuerbach"'[163] – and in which 'government and constitution express the fact that the reality of mankind consists in its labour and activity and not in some abstract political function'[164]: 'how can society be made fully a human instrument, an instrument for developing man and not for suppressing or deluding him?'.[165] Thus the final summary of Marx's development of 'an outlook which was not merely concerned with "interpreting the world in a new way", but directed towards changing it' reads[166]:

There is no sharp break or sudden 'conversion' in his development; he reaches his conclusions not out of petulant distaste or impatient emotion. On the contrary. They grow as a result of powerful and conscientious labour, they rise from deep intellectual and moral roots. It is his ideal of human emancipation, of 'humanism', that inspires him. He hates the fetters that pervert the practical and spiritual life of men, and drives steadily forward to a definition of the barriers that lie in the way of the achievement of 'human society or social humanity' – socialism. This passionate belief in the dignity of man was the abiding inspiration of his work.[167]

The same coupling of 'intellectual and moral roots' characterizes Pascal's introduction of Georg Lukács to the readers of *Studies in European Realism* in the foreword of 1950: 'His social and political experience taught him that the subjectivism and irrationalism of the bourgeoisie, to which he had belonged, are hallucinations which obscure reality and the insistent demands of true humanism.'[168]

---

162 Pascal, 'Karl Marx. His Apprenticeship', p. 3.

163 Roy Pascal, 'Karl Marx: 1843–1943. Political Foundations' (London: Labour Monthly, 1943).

164 Pascal, 'Karl Marx: 1843–1943', pp. 11–12.

165 Pascal, 'Karl Marx: 1843–1943', p. 12.

166 Pascal, 'Karl Marx: 1843–1943', p. 30.

167 Pascal, 'Karl Marx: 1843–1943', p. 29.

168 Pascal, 'Foreword', p. v.

Looking at Pascal's publications prior to 1946 in the previous section, I hope to have shown that Pascal's own reading of the early writings of Marx and Engels in their socio-historical German context on the one hand, and in their European, especially British intellectual context on the other, paved the way for a reading of Lukács which, to a high degree, identified with the Hungarian critic's socio-historical humanist concept of literary criticism. In the final part of my lecture therefore I would like to briefly hint at some lasting effects of the appropriation of Lukács's concept of European Realism in Roy Pascal's later work, even after he left the CPGB.

That Roy Pascal's monographs 'belong to comparative (European) literature' was acknowledged by Claus Bock in his introduction to Pascal's Bithell Memorial Lecture at least as far as *Design and Truth* and *The Dual Voice* are concerned,[169] but Prawer, Hinton Thomas and Forster, in their preface to the 1969 Festschrift, *Essays in German Language, Culture and Society*, include *The German Novel* too,[170] because it 'traced the peculiar course taken by one country against the background of very different traditions in England, France and Russia'.[171] Arrigo Subiotto's British Academy portrayal of Pascal also added *The German Sturm und Drang*[172] as an assessment of 'the significance of the "Sturm und Drang" [...] within a European framework'.[173]

Pascal's *Sturm und Drang* indeed aims at proving: 'Nothing could be more misleading than the thesis that the Sturm und Drang founds a "German movement" which culminated in the rabid nationalists Lagarde, H.S. Chamberlain, Rosenberg, and Hitler.'[174] Accordingly he argues that the Stürmer and Dränger 'remained true to their native experience and circumstances and successfully absorbed the European movement into their own substance'.[175] Pascal demonstrates their 'links [...] with the whole

169   Claus Victor Bock, 'Introduction', in Roy Pascal, *Brecht's Misgivings*. [The 1977 Bithell Memorial Lecture] (London: Institute of Germanic Studies, University of London, 1977), pp. iii-iv (p. iii); Roy Pascal, *Design and Truth in Autobiography* (London: Routledge & Kegan Paul, 1960); Roy Pascal, *The Dual Voice: Free Indirect Speech and its Functioning in the Nineteenth Century European Novel* (Manchester: Manchester University Press, 1977).

170   Roy Pascal, *The German Novel. Studies* (Manchester: Manchester University Press, 1956).

171   Siegbert Salomon Prawer, R. Hinton-Thomas and Leonard Forster, 'Preface', in *Essays in German Language, Culture and Society*, ed. by Siegbert Salomon Prawer, R. Hinton-Thomas and Leonard Forster (London: Institute of Germanic Studies, University of London, 1969), pp. vii-viii (p. vii).

172   Roy Pascal, *The German Sturm und Drang* (Manchester: Manchester University Press, 1953).

173   Arrigo Subiotto, 'Roy Pascal, 1904–1980', *Proceedings of the British Academy*, 67, 1982, 442-57 (p. 452).

174   Pascal, *The German Sturm und Drang*, p. 266.

175   Pascal, *The German Sturm und Drang*, pp. xiii-xvi (p. xv).

tradition of imaginative realism, whether it is in Blake and Wordsworth and Pushkin, or in the realistic novelists like Balzac, Stendhal, and Tolstoy'.[176] Pascal's *The German Novel* was advertised by Manchester University Press as being about 'the peculiarly German type [...] standing apart from the general development' in Europe. Its review in the *Times Literary Supplement*[177] led to a response by the Swiss critic Max Rychner in *Die Zeit*. Rychner turns the Marxist author's thesis that Germany's delayed socio-political development had prevented a German Balzac or Dickens 'in both of whom the two socially highest developed nations find self-enjoyment and self-criticism ingeniously united'[178] against the point made by the *TLS*'s reviewer for whom 'the lack of German novels of international significance testified a lack of love for humanity'.[179] Pascal's many references to Lukács are most frequent in the chapter on Thomas Mann where he expressly follows 'the central thesis of Lukacs'[180] that Mann's work is 'criticism of his times from within the bourgeoisie, not from any point outside'.[181]

In *Design and Truth* Pascal states that his decision to write about autobiography was taken when he was '[t]hinking over recent changes in my thoughts and habits'.[182] He chose 'that of all literary genres which strongestly [*sic*] indicates what is common in the European culture'.[183] There are only four autobiographers who have their own individually titled sub-chapters: Rousseau, Wordsworth, Goethe and Sergey Timofeyewich Aksakoff. The latter was quoted in Pascal's 1950 review of V.G. Belinsky's writings as remembering that in his childhood 'there was not a single high-school

---

176 Pascal, *The German Sturm und Drang*, p. 312.

177 N.A., 'The Hero in German Fiction', *The Times Literary Supplement*, 3 August 1956.

178 Max Rychner, 'Vom deutschen Roman. Anläßlich eines Artikels im Literary Supplement der *Times*', *Die Zeit*, 8 September 1956.

179 Rychner, 'Vom deutschen Roman'. Rodney Livingstone (who in 1971 had started to edit Lukács's political writings) claimed in 1993 that his new edition of *German Realists in the Nineteenth Century* 'illuminate[d] a side of Lukács previously hidden to the English reader, namely his enduring love of German literature' (Rodney Livingstone, 'Introduction', in *Georg Lukács, German Realists in the Nineteenth Century* ed. by R. Livingstone (London: Libris, 1993, p. viii)). Ehrhard Bahr in his 1973 overview of 'The Anglo-Saxon Renaissance of Lukács' called Pascal's appropriation of Lukács' in *The German Novel* 'merely a personal tip' (Ehrhard Bahr, 'Die angelsächsische Lukács-Renaissance', *Text + Kritik*, 30/40, 1973, 70–75 (p. 71).

180 Pascal, *The German Novel*, p. 321.

181 Pascal, *The German Novel*, p. 293.

182 Pascal, 'Preface', in Roy Pascal, *Design and Truth in Autobiography*, pp. vii–ix (p. vii).

183 Roy Pascal, 'Das Abenteuer der Autobiographie', *Welt und Wort*, 20, 1965, 262–63.

teacher who did not know Belinsky's *Letter to Gogol* by heart'.[184] Especially interesting, however, is Pascal's explicit justification for not choosing Maxim Gorki's autobiographical writings because Gorki had 'a wider purpose than the discovery of the self'.[185] But the 'discovery of the self' is, in three chapters, at the centre of Pascal's history of the genre in European literature, moving 'from community to one's own law in oneself'.[186] Here Pascal clearly deviates from Lukács who in *Studies in European Realism* treats Gorki's 'autobiographical writings' as 'follow[ing] the tradition of the old classical autobiographies' 'of Rousseau, Goethe or Tolstoy' in 'their extraordinary objectivity'.[187] Gorki, Lukács writes, 'shows us [...], how a child developed into the mirror of the world'.[188] Although Pascal sets against each other the 'discovery of the self' and the 'acquisition of an outlook',[189] he is willing to accept the latter kind of 'personal subjective history' in some cases, for instance in the case of R.G. Collingwood's *An Autobiography*, written after the 1938 Munich Agreement, which Pascal recommends as 'a most illuminating document of the spiritual situation of the late 1930s',[190] in particular its last chapter. This ends:

> It is not the business of this autobiography to ask how completely the country has in fact been deceived, or how long the present degree of deception will last. I am not writing an account of present political events in England: I am writing a description of the way in which those events impinged upon myself and broke up my pose of a detached professional thinker. I know now that the minute philosophers of my youth, for all their profession of a purely scientific detachment from political affairs, were the propagandists of a coming Fascism. I know that Fascism means the end of clear thinking and the triumph of irrationalism. I know that all my life I have been engaged unawares in a political struggle, fighting against these things in the dark. Henceforth I shall fight in the daylight.[191]

---

184   Roy Pascal, 'The Writer and his Responsibilities', *The Labour Monthly*, 1950, 474–76 (p. 474).

185   Pascal, *Design and Truth*, p. 94.

186   Pascal, 'Das Abenteuer der Autobiographie', p. 262.

187   Lukács, *Studies in European Realism*, p. 221.

188   Lukács, *Studies in European Realism*, p. 226.

189   Pascal, *Design and Truth*, p. 110.

190   Pascal, *Design and Truth*, p. 110.

191   R.G. Collingwood, *An Autobiography* (Oxford: Oxford University Press, 1939), p. 167.

In spite of the reservations he had in principle about autobiographies written by professional politicians, for Pascal the best – and the only – positive 'example' of a political autobiography is Mahatma Gandhi's 'outstanding'[192] *My Own Story*, which at the same time proves that 'members of Eastern civilisations [...] have taken over a European tradition'.[193]

Two years before the German version of *Design and Truth* appeared (the second translation of a monograph by Pascal after *The German Sturm und Drang*), the British Journal of the Congress for Cultural Freedom published an attack on Georg Lukács by George Lichtheim. The impetus for the article was the first publication in English of two books by Lukács, *The Historical Novel* and *The Meaning of Contemporary Realism*, but before a new American edition of *Studies in European Realism* appeared which replaced Roy Pascal's foreword with one by the critic Alfred Kazin. After a defence of Lukács by George Steiner,[194] three of four letters to the editors also opposed Lichtheim's verdict on Lukács's writings as 'an intellectual disaster'.[195] One of them, John Cummings, diagnosed Lukács's habit of 'substitut[ing...] generalisations for a detailed analysis' as 'the inherent disease of his persuasion': '[i]n this he resembles Christopher Caudwell, Alick West, Roy Pascal, Arnold Kettle – to name only a few.'[196] Lichtheim replied by blaming his opponents for 'ignor[ing]' Lukács's 'acceptance' of ‹the intellectual (not merely political) standards of Stalinist middle-brow theorising about culture as well as politics': '[t]here was a time when non-European performances were judged by European criteria. Nowadays the backward countries are beginning to cast their shadow over the more advanced ones.'[197] Lichtheim relies on an imagery which had been worked out for the Congress for Cultural Freedom by Leslie Fiedler to justify the execution of the Rosenbergs, but Lichtheim spells out the racist implication of the construction of an Occident of Western Europe and the USA which, however, culturally refers not to medievalism, but high modernism.[198]

---

192 Collingwood, *An Autobiography*, p. 6.

193 Collingwood, *An Autobiography*, p. 22.

194 'The essential Lukács is contained in *Goethe and His Time, Russian Realism in World Literature, German Realists of the Nineteenth Century, Balzac and French Realism, The Historical Novel*'. George Steiner, 'Georg Lukács and his Devil's Pact', in G. Steiner, *Language and Silence. Essays on Language, Literature and the Inhuman* (New York: Atheneum, 1970), pp. 325–39 (p. 331).

195 Lichtheim, 'An Intellectual Disaster'.

196 John Cumming, letter to the editor; section of 'The Case of Georg Lukács. On George Lichtheim's Controversial Article', *Encounter*, August 1963, 90–96 (p. 94).

197 George Lichtheim, letter to the editor; section of 'The Case of Georg Lukács', p. 96.

198 In 'The Middle Against Both Ends' (*Encounter*, August 1955, 16–23) Fiedler described Ethel and Julius Rosenberg as the epitome of petty bourgeois 'middle brow' Stalinist socialist

All the more remarkable is Roy Pascal's defence of Lukács which centres on the relevance of Marxism for his work on the history of literature: [199]

> [h]is Marxism has made Lukács always see [...] the great aesthetic issue, that most literary critics prudently avoid. [...] he forces us to consider what the relation of art to reality is, and rightly insists that the reality from which art springs is a complex, social-historical nexus, neither separate from man nor merely subjective. [...] hence the [...] interpretations of Shakespeare, Goethe, Balzac, Tolstoy [..] again and again juxtapositions and comparisons are stimulating, enriching.[200]

realism because they were unable to make the clear distinction on the one hand between high avant-garde and low mass culture, on the other hand between facts and fiction; see Andrew Ross, *No Respect. Intellectuals & Popular Culture* (New York: Routledge, 1989), p. 32. Cf. William Pietz, 'The "Post-Colonialism" of Cold War Discourse', *Social Text*, 19/20, 1988, 55–75 (p. 55), who demonstrates how 'four of the most important contributors to the intellectual legitimacy of [anti-totalitarianist] cold war thinking' (George Kennan, George Orwell, Arthur Koestler and Hannah Arendt) 'mapped certain orientalist sterotypes onto the Russians' (Pietz, p. 69), in the main of 'traditional Oriental despotism' (Pietz, p. 79).

199   This defence is ignored by Arpad Kadarkay, *Georg Lukács. Life, Thought and Politics* (Cambridge, MA: Blackwell, 1991), p. 459, who isolates Pascal's treatment of the relationship between Lukács and the Party and thereby misrepresents Pascal's position as '[t]aking a middle road between Lichtheim and Steiner'.

200   Roy Pascal, letter to the Editor; section of 'The Case of Georg Lukács', p. 92.

Recent Bithell Memorial Lectures

2000   A.J. Nicholls, *Fifty Years of Anglo-German Relations*

      ISBN 978 0 85457 197 3   vi, 21pp

2002   **Sigrid Löffler**, *Wer sagt uns, was wir lesen sollen? Die Bücherflut, die Kritik und der literarischer Kanon*

      ISBN 978 0 85457 202 1   vi, 26pp

2004   **Peter von Matt**, *Dichten in der Niemandszeit. Der Lyriker Mörike im leeren Raum zwischen Romantik und Moderne*

      ISBN 978 0 85457 212 0   viii, 20pp

2008   **Peter Stein**, *Schillers 'Wallenstein'-Trilogie auf der Bühne*

      ISBN 978 0 85457 223 6   xii, 16pp

2010   **Matt Frei**, *Berlin. A Clash of Histories. A Personal View*

      ISBN 978 0 85457 232 8   iv, 13pp

2013   **Volker Mertens**, *Die Stimme der Mutter. Thomas Mann und die Musik*

      ISBN 978 0 85457 245 8   vi, 22pp

2015   *English and German Cultural Encounters.* **A.S. Byatt** *in Conversation with Martin Swales and Godela Weiss-Sussex*

      ISBN 978 0 85457 262 5   iv, 16pp

Latest Bithell Series of Dissertations

42   Seiriol Dafydd, *Intercultural and Intertextual Encounters in Michael Roes's Travel Fiction*

ISBN 978 0 85457 242 7   x, 224pp   2015

43   Kim Richmond, *Women Political Prisoners in Germany: Narratives of Self and Captivity, 1915–1991*

ISBN 978 0 85457 247 2   viii, 191pp   2016

44   Katharina Volckmer, *Society and its Outsiders in the Novels of Jakob Wassermann*

ISBN 978 0 85457 250 2   x, 210pp   2016

45   Esther Laufer, *'mit worten lûter unde glanz'*: Metapoetics in Konrad von Würzburg's *'Trojanerkrieg'*

ISBN 978 0 85457 253 3   x, 301pp   2016

46   Marissa Munderloh, *The Emergence of Post-War Hybrid Identities: A Comparative Analysis of National Identity Formations in Germany's Hip-Hop Culture*

ISBN 978 85457 255 7   xi, 245pp   2017